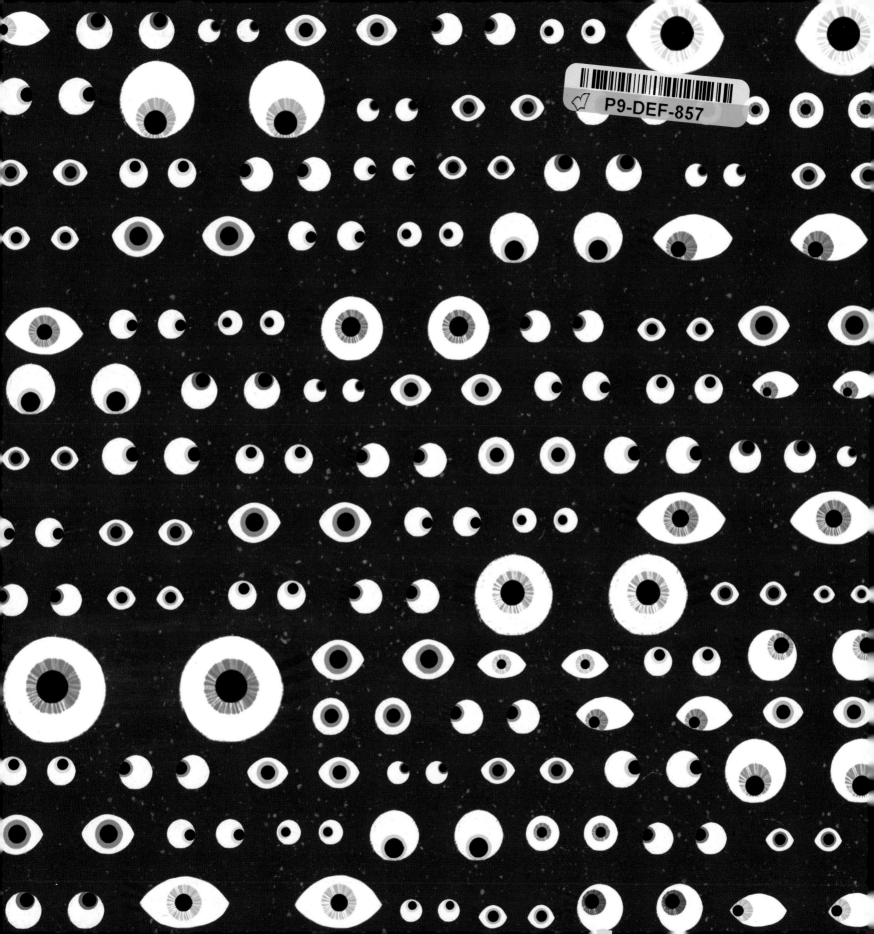

For every child who dares to dream big.
- JFM

For Florence, and thank you Asia
for all your support!
- DR

LCCN 2016961449
ISBN 9781943147311

Text copyright © 2017 by Julia Finley Mosca
Illustrations by Daniel Rieley
Illustrations copyright © 2017 The Innovation Press

Published by The Innovation Press
1001 4th Avenue, Suite 3200, Seattle, WA 98154

www.theinnovationpress.com

Printed and bound by Worzalla
Production Date: May 2017
Plant Location: Stevens Point, Wisconsin

Cover lettering by Nicole LaRue
Cover art by Daniel Rieley
Book layout by Rose Clemens

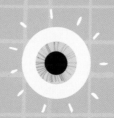

WRITTEN BY
JULIA FINLEY MOSCA

ILLUSTRATED BY
DANIEL RIELEY

THE DOCTOR WITH AN EYE FOR EYES

The Story Of Dr. Patricia Bath

If you like to think BIG,
but some say you're too small,

or they say you're too young
or too slow or too tall . . .

Pay no mind to their doubts,
and just follow the path

of one AWESOME inventor,
PATRICIA E. BATH!

On the fourth of November
in Harlem, New York,

one family, the BATHS,
got a gift from a stork.

A baby! PATRICIA—
quite clever was she.

All the good she'd accomplish,
the world would soon see!

Now, this girl from New York . . .
she loved playing with boys.

Her big brother, so THOUGHTFUL,
shared all of his toys.

Every HOBBY he had,
she would copy. It's true.

She said, "Anything BOYS can do,
GIRLS can do too!"

Yet the toy she loved most—
   she will never forget—

was a gift from her mother:
   a CHEMISTRY SET.

Well, it got her to thinking,
   "Hey, science is NEAT!"

This new passion of hers?
   It just couldn't be beat.

As she grew a bit older,
she yearned to do more.

"With science, I'll HELP
the world's sick and the poor."

And a friend of the family's,
a DOCTOR so swell,

INSPIRED the teen.
"I can be one as well!"

But doctors back then?
Most were men, you will find.

Still, Patricia stood firm.
That did not change her mind.

See, her father was SMART
(and a jack-of-all-trades).

He had taught her:
"We're EQUAL—all genders, all shades."

Yes, her parents were thrilled.
They encouraged her goal.

They said, "Nothing's off limits—
no job, dream, or role."

The Baths didn't have much
but were WISE nonetheless.

"EDUCATION," they said,
"is the KEY to success."

Now, the problem with that?
Every nearby high school . . .

was only for white kids
with money—NOT COOL.

So, to high school by TRAIN.
Nothing stopped her, you see,

and though most kids took four years,
she finished in THREE!

All those unfair restrictions
did not bring her down.

There were more pressing matters
and no time to frown.

A decision was due—
what her FOCUS would be.

"I've been thinking," she said.
"I will help people SEE!"

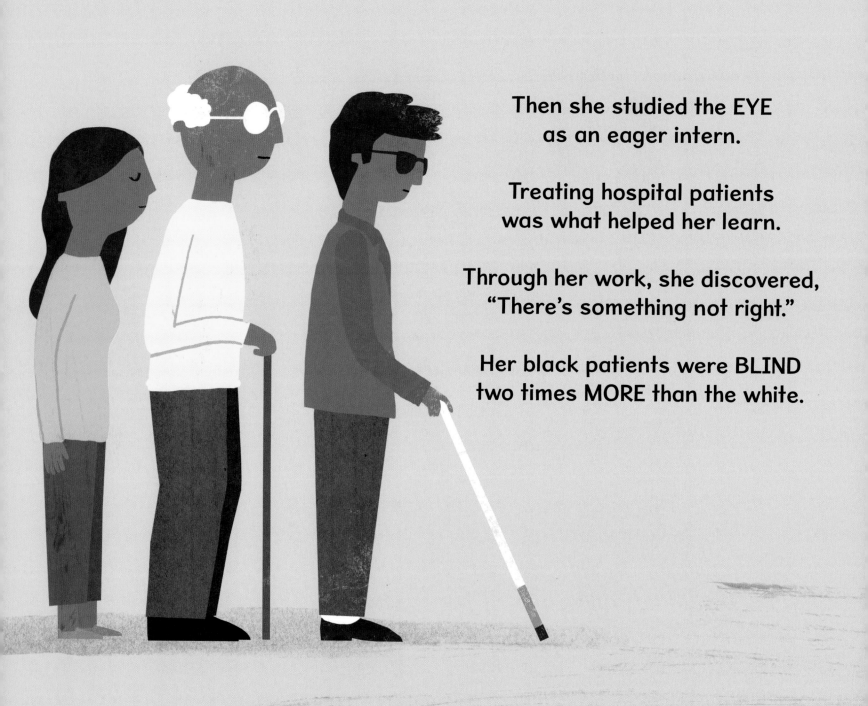

Then she studied the EYE
as an eager intern.

Treating hospital patients
was what helped her learn.

Through her work, she discovered,
"There's something not right."

Her black patients were BLIND
two times MORE than the white.

"What has caused this to happen,"
she wanted to know,

"in locations like Harlem,
where money is low?"

She came up with a plan:
"We must CONQUER this plight.

The public," she said,
"must PRIORITIZE sight!"

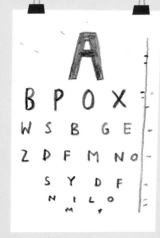

With this MISSION in mind,
the new doctor went west.

At a school near the sea,
she spread word of her quest.

She was young, but her KNOWLEDGE
and SKILL made her wise.

She taught hundreds of students
to understand eyes.

But it wasn't all cheery.
Some things she would FIGHT,

like the desk in a DUNGEON
that barely had light.

"No, thank you," she said.
"I will need a new placement."

'Cause NOBODY puts
Dr. Bath in a basement!

Well, she GOT that new desk.
Then she hit a GRAND SLAM,

when she started an eye
doctor training program.

She would LEAD it for years,
and what makes that so sweet?

She'd be the FIRST WOMAN
to achieve such a feat!

Do you think she stopped there?
No siree, she did not.

All her GOALS to help people?
She still had a lot.

"I will find better TREATMENTS
for blindness," she swore.

Straight to Europe she went,
where she studied some more.

In cities like Paris,
she learned about LASERS.

"These light beams," she said,
"will be little EYE-SAVERS."

She practiced for months.
Oh, and one final mention . . .

Her research? It led her
to make an INVENTION!

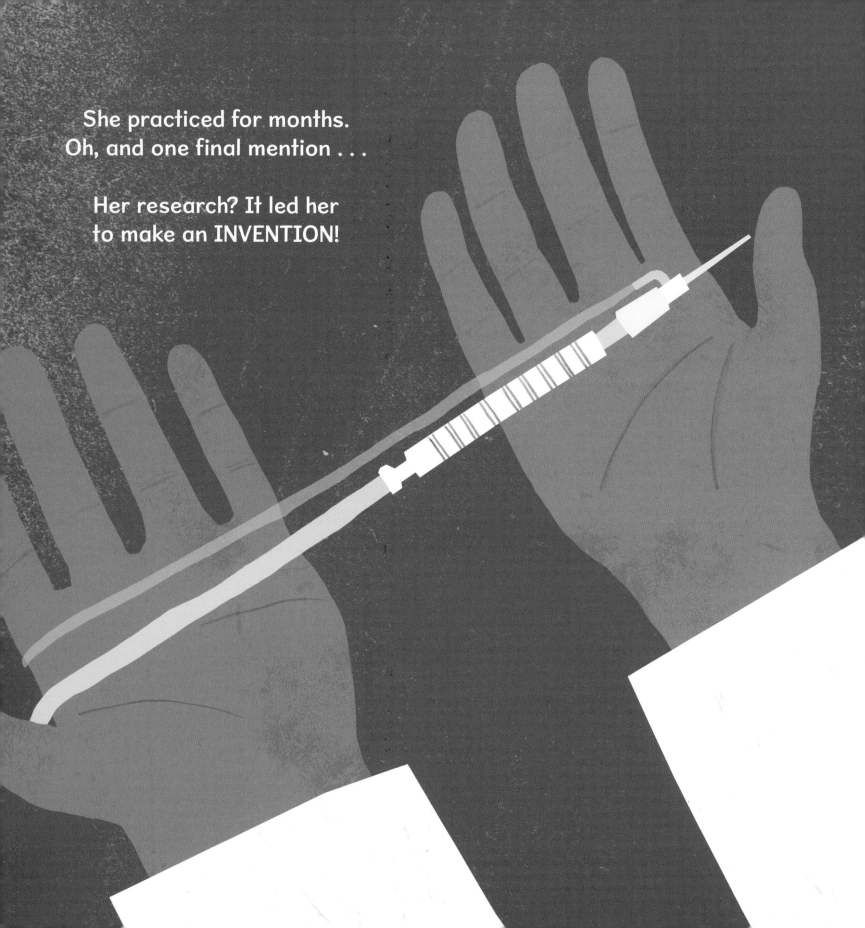

This tool she developed—
a new LASER PROBE—

fixed the EYEBALLS of patients
all over the globe.

And because of her work,
those without sight for years

(like fifteen or twenty
or THIRTY more years) . . .

DR P.BATH

They could finally SEE!
We should give her THREE CHEERS.

HOORAY, Dr. Bath!

HOORAY, Dr. Bath!!

HOORAY, Dr. Bath!!!

AMERICAN INSTITUTE FOR THE PREVENTION OF BLINDNESS

But WAIT! She did more.
She CREATED a place . . .

A place to bring HOPE
to the whole human race.

Its motto is this:
Rich or poor, black or white,

healthy vision's important.
It's everyone's RIGHT!

Now, for all that she's done
and the PROGRESS it brings,

Dr. Bath is well known.
She's accomplished GREAT things.

But applause for her work?
Well, to her, it seems strange.

Fame was never her wish.
What she wanted was CHANGE.

Yes, that girl from New York
with the chemistry set

(who was born when most doctors
were men, don't forget)

grew to be quite a HERO,
but she'll never boast.

It's her will to HEAL people
that matters the most.

So, if helping the world
seems too hard, you are wrong.

If some say you can't do it,
don't listen. Be STRONG.

Like Patricia, stay FOCUSED.
Push FORWARD. Shine BRIGHT . . .

And you'll find all your DREAMS
will be well within SIGHT!

Dear Reader,

Begin each day by asking a question.
Let the answer lead you to another question
and you will discover that learning and knowledge
are an infinite playground.

R_X

Dr. Patricia Bath

FUN FACTS AND TIDBITS FROM THE AUTHOR'S CHAT WITH PATRICIA!

Seeing Beyond Boundaries

As a child, Patricia Bath was never what you might call a girly-girl. "I would play and interact and hang tough with the boys," Bath said, when asked about growing up in Harlem, New York. During these years, her older brother always included and encouraged her. "I thank my brother for sticking up for me. When I wanted to play the male role of the doctor, and not the nurse, he would support that," she said. In fact, Bath believes that having supportive male friends played an important part in her future. "I think that was something which allowed me to have limitless horizons. I was not simply saddled with the games of girls or the toys of girls."

Learning No Limits

Who would have guessed that a simple toy chemistry set would spark a lifelong passion for science? Bath's mother, Gladys, for one—the very person who gave her the gift. "My mom kind of knew I had a curiosity," Bath said. "I was always interested in fixing things, discovering how things were made, or taking things apart." From her father, Rupert, she inherited a deep appreciation for culture. "He worked on oil tanker ships that went all over the world," she explained. "I attribute my internationalism to those early childhood experiences of Dad coming home with [shipmates] from Sweden or Africa or Germany." Yet Bath admits the most important gift her parents ever gave her was a lifelong respect for education. "Mom and Dad felt that education was the ticket to achieve whatever you could dream of, and they were right!"

Eyeing the Possibilities

Perhaps nothing helped young Patricia envision a future in medicine more than two important role models. The first, Dr. Albert Schweitzer, was a white physician who spent decades in West Africa treating people with leprosy and other deadly venereal diseases. "It was very inspiring, especially because of the racial situation in America," she said. "There were whites who didn't want to associate with blacks, and there was segregation in the schools and at the lunch counters. [Dr. Schweitzer] was just an amazing humanitarian, and that really impacted me to see that.'" Someone else who inspired Bath was her very own doctor (also her father's best friend), Dr. Cecil Marquez. "There's a saying: 'You have to see it in order to believe it,'" she explained. "So to have someone in your inner circle—a member of the extended family who was a professional—I think that was important."

Training for Success

If there's one trait that clearly defined Bath's early life, it's perseverance. As a teenager, she learned that African-American girls were not accepted at any of the high schools near her home. "When school would let out, you'd see hundreds of white students, with generally red or blonde hair, right there in the middle of Harlem. So, it was anomalous," she described. Eager to learn, Bath "walked to the subway and hopped on the A train." Each day, she traveled downtown to attend Charles Evans Hughes High School in Manhattan, where she excelled and even graduated early. "I think [an obstacle] just inspires you to kind of reach to your inner strength, since you're not getting a leg up or a boost, and you just have to propel yourself," she said, adding that complications only motivated her to "swim faster, swim harder!"

Breaking All Barriers

Although women attending high school in the 1950s were generally discouraged from pursuing careers in science and technology, Bath was always ahead of her time. "I don't see that there's a reasonable or philosophical barrier, or even a scientific barrier [between sexes] in terms of knowledge and skills," she explained, noting that stereotyping activities as male or female is a learned behavior—one her own family never reinforced. "Luckily, things are changing," she added. "Even the toy manufacturers are beginning to realize that they have a bias if they only have action figures that are boys. I think the movie industry is beginning to recognize that, too, with a lot of the new movies that are featuring girls and women as SHEroes." So, how does all of this make a renowned female doctor feel? For Dr. Bath, the answer is pretty simple: "It's about time!"

1942 Born on November 4th in Harlem, New York

1950 Receives toy chemistry set, sparking an interest in science

1964 Earns bachelor's degree in chemistry from Hunter College in Manhattan

1968 Earns doctoral degree from Howard University College of Medicine

1969 Begins Columbia University fellowship and notices higher rates of blindness in patients of color

1970 Begins three-year residency at NYU; has a daughter, Eraka, during this time

1959 Selected for prestigious National Science Foundation summer program

1960 Wins Mademoiselle magazine's Merit Award for a cancer research project

1967 Travels to Yugoslavia and observes inadequate eye care for the poor

1968 Begins ophthalmology internship at Harlem Hospital Center

1974 Moves to Los Angeles to teach ophthalmology at UCLA and Charles R. Drew University

1993

Named a Howard University Pioneer in Academic Medicine

1988 Elected to the Hunter College Hall of Fame

1993 Retires from UCLA

1977 Co-founds the American Institute for the Prevention of Blindness

1981 Begins researching the idea of lasers to remove cataracts

1986 Travels to Europe to experiment with cutting-edge laser technology

1974 Becomes first full-time female ophthalmologist faculty member in the ophthalmology department at UCLA's Jules Stein Eye Institute

1983 Becomes first US woman to chair an ophthalmology residency program

1986 Completes invention of the Laserphaco Probe

1988 Receives first medical patent for the Laserphaco Probe

Present Lives in Los Angeles, California, where she writes, teaches, and speaks about the importance of eye health as president of the American Institute for the Prevention of Blindness

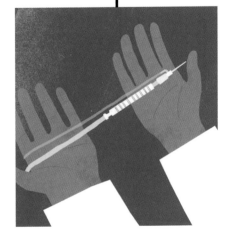

ABOUT DR. PATRICIA BATH

DR. PATRICIA ERA BATH was born in Harlem, New York, on November 4, 1942. Growing up when barriers like sexism, racism, and poverty might have threatened a young African-American girl's dream to be a doctor, Bath fought and succeeded against all odds–making it her life's mission to work for the treatment and prevention of blindness. Today, the accomplished ophthalmologist, inventor, and educator is known and respected around the world.

As a child, Bath and her family lived in a relatively poor section of New York City where children, especially girls, did not often further their education or consider professional careers. Fortunately, Bath's parents encouraged her to aim high and continuously stressed the importance of learning. Her mother, Gladys, worked as a domestic to help finance her schooling, and her father, Rupert, was pivotal in introducing her to different cultures, people, and possibilities. A Renaissance man by all accounts, he toiled as a newspaper columnist, merchant seaman, and one of New York City's first black motormen. It was he who instilled in Bath the importance of equality, even battling racial injustice before the Civil Rights Movement, when he enlisted an attorney (Thurgood Marshall) to help him win the rights to a job he was denied.

In addition to her parents, other individuals inspired Bath at a young age. As a preteen, she learned of Dr. Albert Schweitzer, a well-known doctor, humanitarian, and Nobel Peace Prize winner who treated impoverished victims of leprosy in West Africa. Studying Schweitzer's tireless efforts fueled her desire to help people in need. Meanwhile, the Bath family's physician and friend, Dr. Cecil Marquez, served as an up-close role model in a community where gold-collar professionals were a rarity. When Bath expressed an interest in medicine, her family was supportive—once again, impressing on her the notion that education was the key to achieving this dream.

Unfortunately, attaining that education wasn't so simple. When it came time for high school, Bath was forced to travel outside of her neighborhood because the schools closest to her home were for boys or wealthy white families only. Determined to get her diploma, she took the subway every day to Charles Evans Hughes High School in Manhattan. She was not only admitted to the school, but she excelled, especially in science. A highly gifted student, Bath won numerous honors and recognitions, even earning *Mademoiselle* magazine's Merit Award at the age of 18 for a National Science Foundation research project she conducted on the link between cancer treatment and bionutrients. While still in high school, she also began completing college courses, enabling her to graduate early.

In 1960, Bath enrolled at Hunter College in Manhattan where she had been offered a scholarship. After receiving her bachelor of arts degree in chemistry, she moved to Washington, DC, to begin her doctorate at Howard University College of Medicine. At the time, most doctors and medical students were men, and much to Bath's dismay, female students were often subjected to certain rules and restrictions, such as being banned from sitting in the front row during class. Yet even in the face of discrimination, she did her best to stay focused on the positive aspects of her education. It was at Howard that Bath met an important role model, Dr. Lois A. Young, who was one of the first African-American female ophthalmologists in the country. In fact, she credits Young with inspiring her to specialize in eye and vision care.

Bath finished her doctorate at Howard in 1968, graduating with honors. She then returned to New York to do an internship at Harlem Hospital Center and a fellowship in ophthalmology at Columbia University. While working at Harlem Hospital's Eye Clinic, she began to notice disproportionately high numbers of African-American patients. Her observations led her to conduct a formal study to determine why individuals of that race lost their eyesight at such high rates. Her research resulted in the discovery that blacks had twice the rate of blindness as whites and that blindness due to glaucoma was eight times more frequent. She theorized that the high rates were due to a lack of access to eye care. Because of these findings, Bath developed the medical discipline known as community ophthalmology, which seeks to lower the rate of blindness by providing preventive eye care and treatment to people living in underserved areas.

Following her work as an intern, Bath began a residency in ophthalmology in 1970 at New York University. She finished the program in 1973, making her the first African-American to do so at that school. During her residency, she gave birth to her daughter, Eraka. With her training complete, Bath and her family moved to Los Angeles, California, where she worked briefly as an assistant professor of ophthalmology at two well-known institutions: the Jules Stein Eye Institute at the University of California, Los Angeles (UCLA), and Charles R. Drew University of Medicine and Science.

In 1974, Bath became the first full-time female faculty member in the Department of Ophthalmology at the Jules Stein Eye Institute. Despite this accomplishment, she encountered what she believed to be racial and gender discrimination in the early years of her tenure, including the department's attempt to give her an office in a dark corner of a basement. Never one to be contentious, she simply said the space was unacceptable and asked for professional office space comparable to that of other faculty. Her request was granted, and while Bath agrees that the glass ceiling was still present for much of her career, her perseverance paid off. In 1983, she achieved another impressive feat when she became the first woman in the United States to serve as head of an ophthalmology residency training program, the Charles Drew/UCLA Medical Education Program, which she helped create. During these years of breaking ground in the academic field, she also found time to co-found the American Institute for the Prevention of Blindness, a nonprofit organization dedicated to protecting, preserving, and restoring the gift of sight.

Even with all her success, Bath never lost the urge to find better treatments for blindness. In 1981, she began working on the concept for an invention called the Laserphaco Probe, a device to remove cataracts from the eye using a more effective, less painful method than what was previously used. While on sabbatical from UCLA in the mid-1980s, she traveled to Europe where she spent time researching and working in Paris alongside one of her mentors, Dr. Danièle Aron-Rosa. Bath continued her sabbatical studies at the Free University of Berlin where she had access to some of the best laser equipment in the world, and in 1986 she completed her invention at the university's Laser Medical Center. She received her first patent for the device in 1988 and went on to obtain several more. Many sources have credited her as being the first African-American female doctor to obtain a medical patent in the United States, but Bath has always maintained that the most important result of her work is this: she was the first person (regardless of race or gender) to demonstrate the feasibility of laser cataract removal using a fiber-optic delivery probe combined with irrigation and suction. While we continue to see progress in techniques, Bath will forever be known as a pioneer in laser cataract surgery.

With her revolutionary invention complete, Bath continued to work at UCLA until her retirement in 1993. She still lives in the Los Angeles area today, serving as president for the American Institute for the Prevention of Blindness. It is Bath's belief that over half of all blindness is preventable, and that everyone has the "right to sight." Even in the face of obstacles, she has never given up on this fight.

Throughout her long career, Bath has been honored with many impressive titles, achievements, and awards, yet this humble pioneer will be the first to point out that what really matters is the advancement of science—the discovery of new and better technology and procedures to help the human race. In fact, she has often been quoted as saying, "The ability to restore sight is the ultimate reward." So, while she may or may not agree with the label, it is her genuine selflessness and dedication to humankind that makes Dr. Patricia E. Bath one truly AMAZING SCIENTIST!

Acknowledgements

The publisher, author, and illustrator are immensely grateful to Dr. Patricia Bath for speaking at length with the author, contributing a personal photo, and providing helpful commentary throughout the creation of this book.

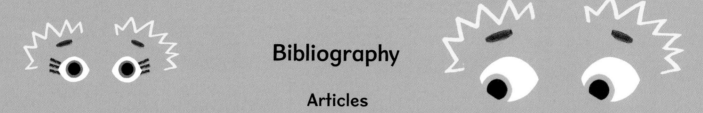

Bibliography

Articles

"Biography of Dr. Patricia E. Bath." *Changing the Face of Medicine.* U.S. National Library of Medicine. June 3, 2015. https://cfmedicine.nlm.nih.gov/physicians/biography_26.html.

"Patricia Bath." *The Black Inventor Online Museum.* November 26, 2012. http://blackinventor.com/patricia-bath.

"The Right to Sight: Patricia Bath." *Innovative Lives.* Smithsonian National Museum of American History. March 3, 2005. http://invention.si.edu/innovative-lives-right-sight-patricia-bath

Bath, Dr. Patricia. Interview by Eve Higginbotham. *Conversation Between Patricia Bath, MD and Eve Higginbotham, MD.* Foundation of the American Academy of Opthamology. October 23, 2011. Print.

Videos/Film

"Women's History Month – Patricia Bath." *Missouri Health.* YouTube. March 16, 2012. https://www.youtube.com/watch?v=cV7PZ9RvhLE.

"Did You Know? Dr. Patricia Bath." *Dare to Dream Network.* YouTube. February 1, 2016. https://www.youtube.com/watch?v=X6yO6H89bN8.

Books

Labrecque, Ellen. *Patricia Bath and Laser Surgery (21st Century Junior Library: Women Innovators)*. Michigan: Cherry Lake Publishing, 2017. Print.

Henderson, Susan K., Fred M. B. Amram, and Margo McLoone. *African-American Inventors III: Patricia Bath, Philip Emeagwali, Henry Sampson, Valerie Thomas, Peter Tolliver (Short Biographies)*. Minnesota: Capstone Press, 1998. Print.

Websites

American Institute for the Prevention of Blindness
http://www.blindnessprevention.org

Laserphaco
http://laserphaco.net